DATE DUE

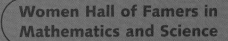

Virginia Apgar

Innovative Female
Physician and Inventor of
the Apgar Score

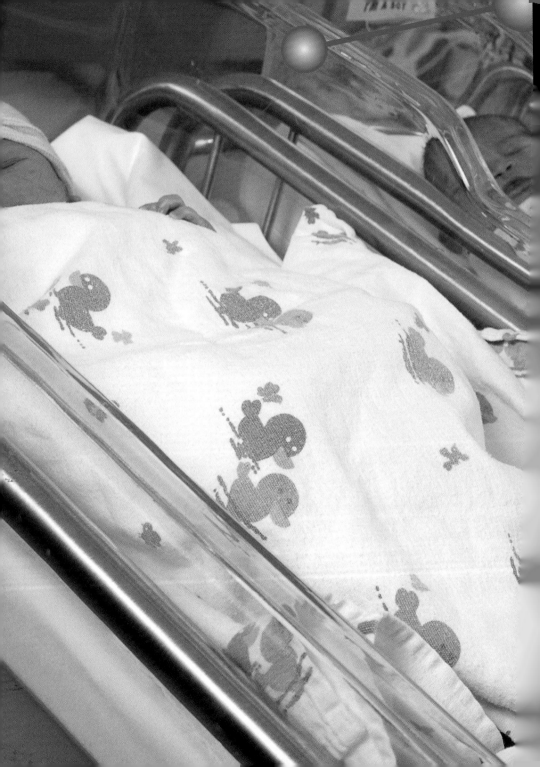

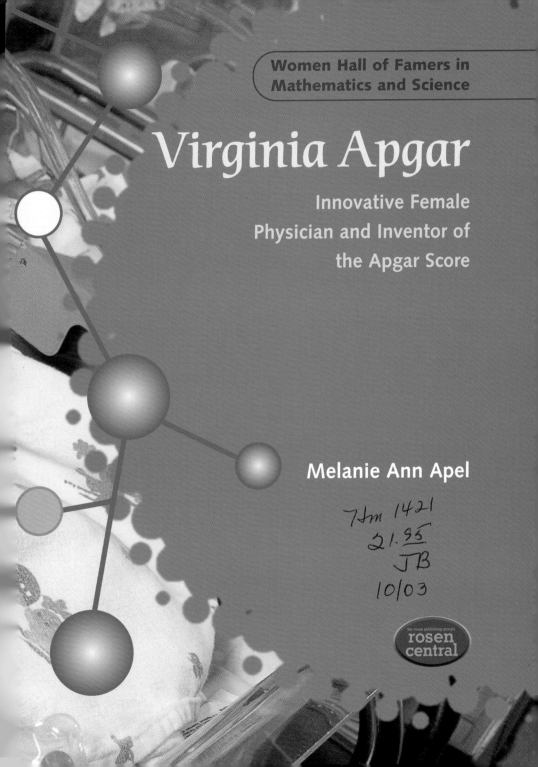

Virginia Apgar

Innovative Female Physician and Inventor of the Apgar Score

Melanie Ann Apel

7tm 1421
21.95
JB
10/03

the rosen publishing group's
rosen
central

This book is dedicated to the strong, accomplished women in my life, all of whom make a difference every day, and not just to me: Jennifer Costin Thomas, Kelly Dimopoulos Lentine, Samantha Hoffman, Esmé Raji Codell, Michele Hammer Ottenfeld, Kathy Christopher French, Lisa Radek Tolnai, Denise Pagel Moskovitz, Dr. Cheryl Gutmann, Dr. Brenda Darrell, my sister, Mindy S. Apel, and, most important, my mother, Carol Apel.

Published in 2004 by The Rosen Publishing Group, Inc.
29 East 21st Street, New York, NY 10010

First Edition

Library of Congress Cataloging-in-Publication Data

Apel, Melanie Ann.
Virginia Apgar : innovative female physician and inventor of the Apgar score / by Melanie Ann Apel.— 1st ed.
    p. cm. — (Women hall of famers in mathematics and science)
Summary: Profiles a woman anesthesiologist who was a pioneer in medicine, graduating from medical school at a time when few women attended college and going on to develop the Apgar score for measuring a newborn's physical condition at birth.
ISBN 0-8239-3880-8 (lib. bdg.)
1. Apgar, Virginia, 1909–1974 —Juvenile literature. 2. Anesthesiologists—United States—Biography—Juvenile literature. 3. Women physicians—United States—Biography—Juvenile literature. 4. Apgar score—History—Juvenile literature. [1. Apgar, Virginia, 1909–1974. 2. Anesthesiologists. 3. Physicians. 4. Scientists. 5. Women—Biography. 6. Apgar score.] I. Title. II. Series.
RD80.62.A64 A64 2003
617.9'6'092—dc21

                                                    2002009415

Manufactured in the United States of America

Contents

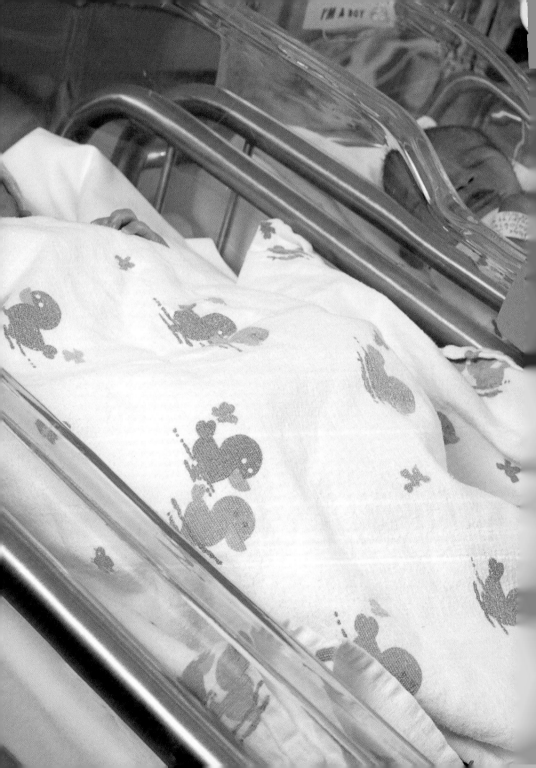

Introduction

Thirty years after her death, Dr. Virginia Apgar is known as a legend, a trailblazer, and an inventor. In 1994, she became one of only two American anesthesiologists to be honored by having her portrait printed on a U.S. postage stamp. The twenty-cent Virginia Apgar stamp shows a warm, friendly face behind grandmotherly looking glasses and silver hair. Virginia Apgar was only the third female doctor to be pictured on a U.S. postage stamp. On October 14, 1995, almost a year to the day after the postage stamp was released, Virginia Apgar was inducted into the National Women's Hall of Fame in Seneca Falls, New York.

Who was Virginia Apgar and what did she do that was so important to merit her face on a postage stamp and a place in the National Women's Hall of Fame?

Virginia Apgar was a woman who was far ahead of her time. She entered the medical field and became a doctor during a time when many women did not even go to college. She was a strong and independent woman who accomplished a great deal and achieved remarkable things in her lifetime. Because of her important work, she received honors from many different groups both during her lifetime and after her death. The greatest measure of her achievements is the fact that today, almost thirty years after she died, doctors and nurses are still using the Apgar score on every baby born in the United States. The Apgar score is a measure of a baby's health after birth, and it was Virginia's creation.

Virginia Apgar was a remarkable woman and a role model to women not only in her day, but to today's women as well. She has been called a legend for her remarkable achievements, which affect us to this day. She has been called a trailblazer for creating a path for other women to follow. She has even been called an inventor for her creation of the Apgar score. Those who knew her personally called her Ginny.

1

Virginia Apgar's Early Years

Summer was just getting started in Westfield, New Jersey, on June 7, 1909, the day on which Virginia Apgar was born. Her parents, Helen Clarke Apgar and Charles Emory Apgar, were thrilled to welcome their new baby daughter to their family and to the world. The Apgars already had two sons. Their first little boy was named Charles Emory Apgar Jr., after his father. Unfortunately, little Charles died of tuberculosis before he reached his fourth birthday, not an uncommon fate for a young person living in the early 1900s. Their second son, Lawrence Clarke Apgar, was two years old when Ginny was born. The

Apgars had high hopes for their new baby girl, but they had no idea that she would grow up to accomplish so much.

Charles Apgar worked as a salesman for the New York Life Insurance Company. He was also an executive for Spencer Trask & Co., a company that invests money in remarkable inventions and scientific discoveries. Mr. Apgar was fascinated by science in general and by astronomy in particular. He even built his own telescope right in the Apgar family's basement. As a hobby, he wrote many articles for the Royal Canadian Astronomical Society, including a few scientific papers on the moons of Jupiter.

Virginia's father was an extremely intelligent and creative man. His love of science was something that he shared with his young daughter. He accomplished some fairly exciting things in his lifetime, which set a great example for Virginia.

VIRGINIA'S FATHER CRACKS THE CODE

Charles Apgar was also very interested in the radio, and he performed experiments with electric-

Virginia had a lot to smile about. Her childhood hobbies and experiences helped shape her into a very important and well-respected woman. Her interest in science and dealing with her sibling's sickness and untimely death made Virginia want to become a doctor. Her love of music also stayed with her throughout her life.

ity and radio waves in a laboratory that he had set up in the basement. In the early 1900s, radio was not what it is today—it was used to send messages, not to listen to music. In 1915, Mr. Apgar owned and operated one of the most powerful receiving sets in the country. During World War I, the U.S. War Department suspected that messages were being sent from a German station at Sayville, Long Island. German U-boats were disrupting Allied shipping in the Atlantic Ocean. A German-subsidized radio station at Sayville was suspected of relaying vital sailing dates of U.S. convoys to the German high command. These suspected messages were in a secret code. The War Department could not track the messages to decipher the secret code. For fun, Mr. Apgar practiced translating the messages sent out from the Sayville towers. One night, he noticed something strange about the messages. When the radio station operator in Long Island and the radio station operator in Germany finished their official business, they talked to each other for a few more minutes. Although Mr. Apgar did not know exactly what this meant, he made records of these chats and sent them to Secret Service headquarters each morning.

To the War Department's surprise and delight, Mr. Apgar helped to trace the messages and crack the code to discover the meaning of the messages that were being transmitted to German submarines about the movements of neutral ships in the area.

The radio station that had been sending these messages was dismantled. Thanks to the work of Virginia's father, U-boats stopped sinking Allied ships, and the German wireless operator was sent to the federal prison at Atlanta.

MUSICAL APGARS

Another of Mr. Apgar's hobbies was music. As an amateur musician, he often held concerts for his family right in their own living room. Charles Apgar passed this hobby on to his children. Both Virginia and her brother began music lessons when they were very young. Starting violin lessons at the age of six, Virginia spent a lot of her time learning to play both the violin and the cello.

Virginia's brother Lawrence played the piano. When the two were a bit older, it was their turn to put on concerts in the living room. Their audience was, of course, their parents. The Apgar kids were pretty serious about their music, even though they were young. Virginia's great-nephew still has some of the programs from the Apgar kids' performances. One program, from March 1922, lists both children in a violin recital at the Westfield Theatre given by the pupils of Josephine MacKenzie. Twelve-year-old Virginia played violin and fifteen-year-old Lawrence accompanied the violinists on the piano.

A PREVIEW OF A LIFE IN MEDICINE

Virginia's mother stayed at home and took care of Virginia and her brother, as women in the early 1900s were expected to do. When Virginia's brother Lawrence was a child he suffered from chronic eczema. Eczema is a condition in which the skin is continually red, itchy, and covered in scaly or crusted spots. Lawrence's eczema was chronic, meaning it came and went over a long period of time. Because of his condition, Lawrence spent most of his time with his mother. Probably because Mrs. Apgar was often busy taking care of her sick son, Virginia spent a lot of time with her father. Their interests were similar and they truly enjoyed each other's company. Virginia spent hours with her dad playing music, working on scientific experiments, or looking at the stars through his homemade telescope.

Virginia was a smart girl. In high school, she studied higher mathematics and Greek. She collected stamps (a hobby that she would continue throughout her life). She was on the high school debate club for four years. Tall, thin, and athletic, she found time to play both tennis and basketball all four years of high school, as well as run with the track team. And, of course, she played in the high school orchestra for four years. After finishing high school, she wanted to do something that most girls of her time did not do. Rather than get married and start a family right away, Virginia wanted to go to college. In fact, she already knew that she wanted to become a doctor. No one knows exactly why Virginia was so determined to become a doctor. At the time, it was highly unusual for a woman to want to go into medicine. Virginia had never even met a female doctor before. Perhaps her desire to become a doctor resulted from both of her brothers having suffered from illnesses. Although she had never met her brother Charles Jr., Virginia had heard people talk about him and how he had died of tuberculosis. Perhaps a combination of hearing those stories and visiting Lawrence's doctor with him so often influenced her decision. Perhaps it was just another thing Charles Apgar passed down to his daughter: an interest in science.

MOUNT HOLYOKE COLLEGE

In 1925, Virginia entered Mount Holyoke College in South Hadley, Massachusetts. She majored in zoology, the field of biology that deals with animals and animal life. She minored in chemistry. Virginia was

Virgina graduated from Mount Holyoke with a bachelor of arts degree. During her years at Mount Holyoke, which is located in South Hadley, Massachusetts, she was involved in many extracurricular activities, such as orchestra and the-ater. She left the beautiful campus, pictured here, in 1929 and headed to New York.

Hadley, Mass.

very active on the college campus. She continued to play both the cello and the violin. She even found time to play her violin in Mount Holyoke's orchestra. She also acted in several of the school's plays. Virginia did well at Mount Holyoke, and in 1929 she was ready to graduate.

Although she had just received her bachelor of arts degree from Mount Holyoke, Virginia was broke. She had no money to live on. Scholarships had paid her tuition. Scholarship students are often expected to work on the college campus to help pay their tuition. They are sometimes given first choice of the available jobs on campus. Virginia had taken several odd jobs to support herself. One of those jobs was in the laboratory of the zoology department. The job sounds like something that might have helped further her career, but it did not—her job was to catch stray cats for the lab! The cats would be euthanized, or painlessly killed, and then preserved. Students studying zoology at Mount Holyoke would then dissect the cats as part of their classwork.

COLUMBIA UNIVERSITY'S COLLEGE OF PHYSICIANS AND SURGEONS

After college, Virginia was still determined to work in the field of medicine. She enrolled in Columbia University's College of Physicians and Surgeons. She was granted a few scholarships, but they were not enough to pay for school entirely. She had to borrow the rest of her tuition money from friends of her family. When Virginia graduated in 1933, she was fourth in her class. She was also a member of Alpha Omega Alpha, the only national medical honor society in the world, which was founded in 1902.

Virginia already had some decent achieve-ments under her belt, but times were tough. America was in the middle of the Great Depression, and Virginia was in debt, owing almost $4,000. But Virginia knew that good things were ahead. By this time, Virginia had earned the right to add the letters "M.D." to the end of her name. At age twenty-four, Virginia Apgar was a doctor!

2

Becoming a Doctor: Internships and Beyond

Before Virginia could see patients of her own, she first had to do her internship and residency. These are the steps all doctors take before they become full-fledged doctors. Virginia had decided that she would become a surgeon. Following her 1933 graduation from Columbia University's College of Physicians and Surgeons, she was very lucky to win a spot at Columbia Presbyterian Hospital for her surgical internship. She stayed on there to do her residency as well. Her work was impressive, to say the least, but despite this, Virginia would not become a surgeon after all.

After Virginia spent two years learning about and working in surgery, Dr. Alan Whipple, the chairman of surgery, told her that he did not think it would be a good idea for her to continue in the field of surgery. He explained his reasons to Virginia. There were already a large number of surgeons in New York City. Dr. Whipple said that other female surgeons had experienced some trouble starting their own surgical practices. Things would be even more difficult for a woman because of the Great Depression. Even the men were having trouble, he told her. Virginia was not married and she did not have much money of her own. How would she support herself and pay off her debts if she could not find a job?

Dr. Whipple did think she should stay in medicine, however. He felt that because she was so bright and so determined to do well, she would have a good chance of success if she switched to another field. Dr. Whipple suggested Virginia become an anesthesiologist. At the time, anesthesiology was not as advanced as it is today. Dr. Whipple realized that in order to make anesthetic medicine

After college, Virginia attended Columbia University's College of Physicians and Surgeons. The school was affiliated with Columbia Presbyterian Hospital, where Virginia learned anesthesiology from the nurses. The two buildings were adjacent to each other.

better, there would have to be better anesthesiologists. Few doctors actually specialized in anesthesiology at the time, and the duties of anesthesiology usually fell to nurses. Nurse anesthetists, as these nurses were called, had been assisting doctors in American operating rooms since the 1880s. They were reliable and patient, and they had the technical skills they needed to do their jobs well. They were well respected.

Another reason for Dr. Whipple's suggestion was that, at the time, many academic surgeons were worried about the future of surgery. They did not think that they would have any chance of advancing their surgical techniques unless someone came along who could help to develop better anesthetic medicines. Dr. Whipple felt that Virginia was smart enough and had enough energy and ability to be one of the people who could help to change the field of anesthesiology and improve surgical techniques. Dr. Whipple suspected that Virginia would make a significant contribution to anesthesiology. Virginia respected Dr. Whipple and decided to take his advice. She was very glad that she did, and so was the world of medicine.

WHAT IS ANESTHESIOLOGY?

For several reasons, when a person has an operation, it is very important that he or she is asleep during the surgery. One reason is to minimize pain. The other reason is to keep the person perfectly still so the surgeon can perform the operation delicately and precisely. Just going to sleep on your own is not enough. In order to make sure that you do not wake up or feel the pain, you are given some medicine to help you sleep through the operation. This medicine is called an anesthetic. Anesthetic medicine relaxes your body and puts you to sleep until the operation is over.

Any medicine that keeps you asleep through a painful operation has to be pretty strong. Such strong medicine could be very dangerous if the person giving it to you did not know exactly how much to give you. That is why doctors with the responsibility of giving anesthetics during operations have to have special training. They are called anesthesiologists.

The anesthesiologist is responsible for the patient's life. He or she must know important things about the patient, such as his or her age, weight, height, and medical history. The anesthesiologist also must know what type of operation the patient is going to have and how long it is expected to last. Using this information, the anesthesiologist calculates just the right amount of anesthetic for the patient. If he or she does not give enough of the anesthetic, the patient will wake up in the middle of the operation. If too much anesthetic is given, the patient may never wake up at all.

The anesthesiologist pays very close attention to the patient during the operation. He or she must watch how fast the patient is breathing and how fast the patient's heart is beating. Today there are machines to do the actual counting of the breaths and the heartbeats. But the anesthesiologist still has to watch those machines, called monitors, to be sure that the patient's breathing rate and heart rate are normal throughout the operation. If something is not right, the anesthesiologist must fix it, and fast. This kind of work is only good for a very responsible, detail-oriented person.

LEARNING FROM NURSES

Anesthesiology was an up-and-coming field in the 1930s. This means that, although it had existed before, it had not been a specialty of doctors. It had been part of the job that nurses performed, so nurses taught Virginia to do her job.

Virginia had only just begun her surgical internship when she decided that Dr. Whipple might have been right about her switching from surgery to anesthesiology. She decided to give it a try. Virginia began her search for training in anesthesia in August 1934. This was a time long before the Internet and even telephones as we know them. Searches for information were made the old-fashioned way: with paper and pen. Virginia wrote a letter to Dr. Frank McMechan. Dr. McMechan was the secretary-general of the Associated Anesthetists of the United States and Canada, which was the major North American anesthesia organization at that time. Virginia asked Dr. McMechan to send her a list of all available training positions. Dr.

McMechan wrote back that there were thirteen training institutions in the United States and Canada. He mentioned that the length of training at these institutions varied from just two weeks to three years. Only two of the programs paid salaries.

Virginia decided that her best bet was to stay on at Columbia and finish her surgical internship. She still wanted to make the switch to studying anesthesia, but she was not sure what to do about the limited number of programs that paid a salary. So she stayed at Columbia and finished up her surgical internship in November 1935. Then she decided that she ought to stay at Columbia even longer. Still concerned that only two of the anesthesia programs in the country offered any sort of pay, Virginia probably could not afford to leave Columbia, where she was getting paid to work. She would have to find another way to learn anesthesiology.

From 1936 to 1937, Virginia learned the basics of anesthesiology from the nurse anesthetists at Columbia Presbyterian Hospital. On

January 1, 1937, she took a trip to Madison, Wisconsin. She planned to get more training by visiting the department of anesthesia headed by Dr. Ralph Waters. Dr. Waters's anesthesia department had been the first of its kind in the United States. It was also the most important one. Virginia spent six months in Madison. Once again, being a woman in a man's world, she encountered problems. Her biggest problem was that she had no place to live. Housing for doctors working in Madison hospitals was only for men. There was no housing for the female doctors. Virginia moved three times in six months. Finally, she went back to New York City. She spent the next six months with Dr. Ernest Rovenstine at Bellevue Hospital. Dr. Rovenstine was a graduate of the Madison program. Again Virginia had problems finding a decent place to live. This time she ended up making a temporary home in the maids' quarters in the clinic building of Bellevue. Virginia was getting a little bit tired of everything in the medical world revolving around men. She felt left out. She did not like the fact that although she was accepted at serious things like meetings, she was not invited to join the men for a fun dinner afterwards.

LEADING THE WAY

In 1938, Virginia finished her anesthesiology residency at Bellevue. She went back to Columbia Presbyterian Hospital to work in the division of anesthesia. The following year, she became the second woman ever to receive her board certification from the American Society of Anesthesiologists. Although she was new to the field, the field itself was fairly new and it needed a leader. Who better to become its leader than Virginia Apgar? During the same year, Virginia was appointed anesthesiologist-in-chief of the division of anesthesia at Columbia Presbyterian Hospital. In a style that would become typical of Virginia throughout her career, she became the first woman to head a department at Columbia

VIRGINIA APGAR

Presbyterian. Although she was merely thirty years old and had only just begun her career, Virginia Apgar was already blazing a new trail for women.

3

A Working Woman

By 1949, Virginia Apgar had decided to specialize her medical skills further. She would move into the medical field that would lead to her greatest professional achievements. She had decided to become an obstetric anesthesiologist. This meant that she would work in the delivery room alongside obstetricians and nurses who delivered babies.

Anesthetic medicine is often given to women for normal deliveries. For different reasons, some women do not have any anesthetic when they have a baby. But a large number of women choose to have some anesthetic so that they are numb from the waist down while they give birth, because childbirth is a painful process. Women are still awake to deliver their babies, but they do not feel the worst of the pain. Most women only feel pressure and a small amount of pain. Without anesthetic, having a baby can be very painful.

IN THE DELIVERY ROOM

Before Virginia's time, anesthetic was not commonly used in the delivery room, and many mothers suffered terribly while giving birth. Virginia would change all that.

Virginia's new job would put her on hand in the operating room for cesarean section deliveries as well. There, she would be sure that mothers giving birth to babies by cesarean section had the right kind and the right amount of anesthetic.

Deciding to become an obstetric anesthesiologist was a smart choice for Virginia, and her timing could not have been better. At the time, not much was written about obstetric anesthesiology and not many anesthesiologists were choosing to work in the field of obstetrics. More obstetric anesthesiologists were badly needed. In New York City, where Virginia worked, doctors had a problem on their hands. Many mothers were dying during or just after giving birth to their babies. Something had to be done about this problem.

C-SECTIONS EXPLAINED

Cesarean section—or C-section, as it is commonly called today—is when the abdomen of a pregnant woman is surgically cut open and the baby is delivered through the incision. Doctors deliver babies by C-section for many different reasons. The baby may be too big to be delivered naturally. The mother may be too sick to deliver it normally. The baby may be in distress (if its heart rate drops too low, for example). These are just a few examples of reasons for having a C-section. Most women do not have C-sections when giving birth to their babies. Most babies are born vaginally, that is, they pass through the vaginal canal and come out through the vaginal opening. But for the women who do need C-sections, anesthetic is very important.

VIRGINIA THE TEACHER

A study was done at Columbia Sloane Hospital for Women just before Virginia started working there. By the time Virginia got there, things were already in place for helping to improve the health of pregnant women. Virginia stepped right in and worked hard to do as much as she could.

Virginia's work toward becoming an obstetric anesthesiologist was interrupted briefly in 1950 by a very sad occasion: Virginia's father died. Although Virginia lost a good friend when her father passed away, she was at least comforted by the knowledge that he had lived to see her become a doctor.

Right from the start Virginia had a great influence on the field of obstetric anesthesiology. Anesthesia residents, the young doctors who were training to become anesthesiologists, were finally deciding to go into obstetric anesthesiology. Some of them just wanted the opportunity to get to work with Virginia. In order to do so, many of them chose to do obstetrics rotations. Virginia was their teacher.

Virginia used her knowledge of anesthesia to work in the field of obstetric anesthesiology. She took great care to keep a good watch on the newborns to see how different anesthetics affected infants. She wanted to ensure that the babies were not harmed by the anesthesia.

Her teaching style was very informal. Virginia preferred to take a real-life approach rather than to give her students a classroom lecture. Sometimes she would give lessons right at the bedsides of her patients. Other times she gathered her students in the hospital hallway to give them a lesson. Virginia was well known for being an enthusiastic, outgoing teacher. It is no wonder that residents wanted to learn from Virginia.

Virginia could not give her students very much reading homework. Obstetric anesthesiology was so new that not much had been written about it yet. Instead, Virginia used a variety of teaching tools that might have been considered somewhat off-the-wall. But her teaching tools made learning interesting, and her students were sure to remember what she taught them. She used an old, battered pelvis bone and a skeleton to give demonstrations. If what she needed was more than these bones could offer, she used her own body as an example, often pointing to places where anesthesia should be administered. By 1955, Virginia was the head of the obstetric anesthesia department.

WATCHING THE BABIES

After Virginia made the switch from anesthesiologist to obstetric anesthesiologist, she spent a great deal of time watching and studying babies, especially newborn babies. Obstetrics is the area of medicine that deals with women during pregnancy, childbirth, and the period right after giving birth. Virginia got to see a lot of newborn babies. While she was working, Virginia was also studying and learning. She watched to see what happened when anesthetic agents were used on pregnant mothers. More specifically, she watched the affects of anesthesia on unborn babies (called fetuses). One thing she found was that one of the anesthetics commonly used on mothers giving birth was causing their babies to have problems breathing. When she proved that she was right about this, that anesthetic was no longer used in the delivery room. She also discovered that mothers could have a local anesthetic—one that only numbs a certain area—while giving birth rather than having general anesthesia, which put the mother to sleep until

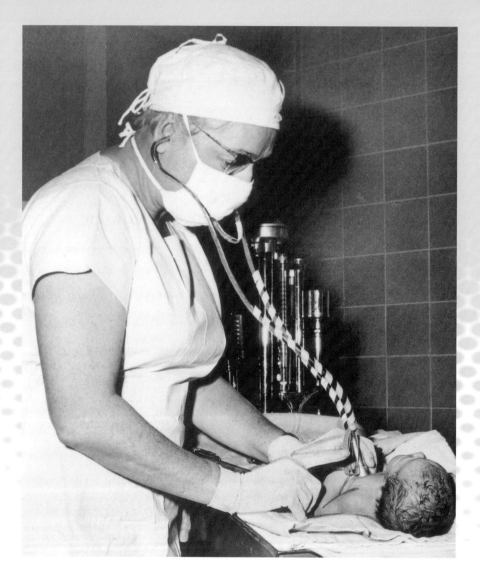

Virginia dedicated her life's work to helping infants. She is most remembered for her Apgar score, which measures a newborn's well-being after birth. Although Virginia loved working with babies, she never had any of her own.

after the baby was born. One of the best things about this discovery was that women were finally awake and able to enjoy the beauty of giving birth. They also got to see their babies right away, the minute they were born. Usually, women had to wait until they had woken from the anesthetic before they could see their babies.

Virginia was very observant and willing to experiment (though never causing harm to the babies or their mothers, of course). She learned many very important things that changed the way babies are taken care of today. One of the most important things that she noticed had to do with infant resuscitation, which is simply helping new-born babies breathe if they do not start to do so on their own. Virginia noticed that infant resuscitation was not well understood, and that there was no standard way of performing it. Many strange and unusual methods were used.

Dr. L. Stanley James, one of Virginia's colleagues, later said about Virginia during this period of her career:

Virginia was not just a doctor. She was also an educator. Whenever she figured out something new about babies and how to best care for them right after they were born, she made sure to teach her new information to as many doctors as she possibly could. Sometimes this meant giving lectures. Other times this meant making short films to distribute to doctors all over the U.S.

Another thing that Virginia noticed while she was working as an obstetric anesthesiologist was that newborn babies were too often being neglected in the delivery room. Not only were the methods of resuscitating newborns bad, but the methods doctors used to check the babies after they were born were also bad. Doctors and nurses had a bad habit of checking out newborn babies in ways that were inconsistent and somewhat dangerous. She noticed that their methods were not at all scientific. To Virginia's brilliant and compassionate mind, this was a completely unacceptable way for babies to begin life. Luckily for the babies to come, things were about to change.

4

The Apgar Score

Virginia Apgar certainly had a great many accomplishments during her life. However, at this point, she had never worked as a pediatrician (a doctor who specializes in the care of children) or as an obstetrician (a doctor who specializes in the care of pregnant women and delivers babies). Yet the one thing she is most remembered for, the accomplishment that even today still bears her name, has to do with babies and their transition from the end of pregnancy to the first moments of life. Virginia Apgar is most famous for the Apgar score.

AN IDEA OVER BREAKFAST

One morning in 1949, Virginia was sitting in the cafeteria of the hospital where she worked. As she ate breakfast, one of her medical students stopped by. The student wanted to know if there was a correct way to evaluate newborn babies. Virginia's experience in obstetric anesthesiology had prepared her well for this moment. Virginia is said to have told the medical student, "That's easy. You do it this way." Then, using the back of a notice that told people to bus their own cafeteria trays, Virginia wrote down the five important points to look for in a newborn. She wrote it in a way that was a system for giving a newborn a score. The medical student thanked Virginia, took the paper, and was on his way. Eager to try out her new idea, Virginia hurried up to the obstetrics department to try it out for herself. It is no surprise that Virginia's idea worked. What Virginia wrote down for the medical student would become the famous Apgar score.

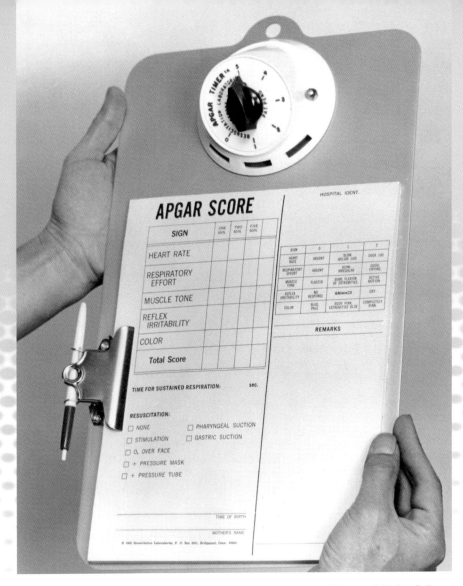

In 1953, the Newborn Scoring System was first published. It was later revised to the Apgar score. Both of these methods involved evaluating newborns to figure out how healthy they were right after being born. This document outlines the five signs that are a part of the Apgar score.

EVALUATING NEWBORNS

Imagine a mother giving birth to a baby. After nine months of pregnancy and then hours of labor, struggling to get the baby out, the mother is exhilarated by the sight of her tiny, precious newborn. The mother looks at her new baby through tears of joy. Beside mother and child, the baby's father is also crying with happiness at the sight of his beautiful new baby. But is everything really as perfect as the new parents believe?

Before Virginia Apgar created her now famous Apgar score, newborn babies did not often get the attention they needed just after they were born. Too often, the nurses and doctors would look at a new baby similar to the way its parents did, seeing just a beautiful newborn, and declare it healthy. The baby would then be whisked off to the nursery where it was weighed and measured, washed, and foot-printed. Everything seemed to be just fine with the baby. But too often, everything was not fine. Shortly after birth, many babies would seem to develop a problem suddenly. Perhaps the baby would stop breathing and turn blue. Or perhaps some time would go by and suddenly the baby would seem extremely sick. Doctors would rush into the nursery and do all they could to figure out what was wrong with the baby and see whether they could do anything to fix the problem. All too often, it was too late and the baby, who had seemed so perfect at birth, died. Had there been a system in place to make sure doctors and nurses checked important things, such as heartbeat and breathing pattern from the moment a baby was born, many of these babies would probably not have died.

From the quick scratchings on the back of the cafeteria notice, Virginia developed the Apgar score, a scoring system for newborns. By using the Apgar score, doctors and nurses in the delivery room would be able to tell whether a baby needed resuscitation or other special care right away, instead of when it was already too late. The Apgar score also helped doctors to figure out why many babies were not born healthy and did not live long after birth.

When a baby is born, its measurements are taken right away. The height, weight, and time of birth are carefully checked and written down. Aside from the baby's name, these are the statistics everyone is so eager to find out about the baby. Thanks to Virginia, other things are checked right away, too. Every baby is given an Apgar score to tell just how well he or she is doing right after being born.

Newborn Scoring System

The first few moments of a baby's life are very important. What happens at this time can often affect the rest of the baby's life. Virginia understood this. In fact, she felt that being born was the most dangerous time in a person's life. She wanted to be sure that all babies had a good chance of getting any medical attention they might need right away. Before 1949, all babies were considered healthy unless some obvious health problem appeared, like a serious breathing difficulty or some type of physical defect. Unfortunately, this assumption caused problems. Many babies had problems that were not so easy to see right away. Sometimes babies died because their problems were not noticed and therefore not taken care of right away.

At first, Virginia's test was called the Newborn Scoring System. The test measures the newborn's physical condition in the minutes right after being born. At one minute after birth and again at five minutes after birth, the baby gets a score for five different signs. The baby is scored one more time, at ten minutes after birth, if any problems show up in the first two tests. For each sign, a baby can get zero, one, or two points. Two is the highest score on each sign. Therefore, the highest overall score a baby can get is a perfect ten. A score of seven to ten is considered normal. A score of four to six means that the baby might need some help with its breathing and its heartbeat. A baby who scores a three or below on the Apgar score will need major help right away if he or she is to survive.

Virginia's Newborn Scoring System was first presented at a meeting in 1952. Unfortunately, as with many new things, the Newborn Scoring System did not catch on right away. Eventually, though, it was accepted and it was published in 1953. It was not until nearly ten years later, however, that Virginia's Newborn Scoring System was officially given the name "Apgar score." In 1962, two pediatricians from the University of Colorado Medical Center came up with an acronym using Virginia's last name. The doctors assigned one newborn assessment for each letter of the name Apgar, using simple words to help users remember what to look for. The words Appearance, Pulse, Grimace, Activity, and Respiration (APGAR) and their definitions made it easy to remember what to look for in a newborn when using the Apgar score.

AN EXPLANATION OF THE APGAR SCORE

The acronym APGAR was reported in the *Journal of the American Medical Association* in 1963. This acronym helped to teach doctors and nurses how to use the scoring system by using the letters of Virginia's last name. A doctor named L. Joseph Butterfield helped to create and is credited for this acronym. Each letter of Virginia's last name stands for a sign in the test.

A stands for Appearance. The doctor or the nurse looks at the baby's color. If the baby's color is normal, it receives a score of two. If the color is normal on most of the body, but the hands and feet look pale or blue, it receives a score of one. If the baby is blue or gray or its whole body is pale, it receives a score of zero.

P stands for Pulse. Your pulse is the measurement of how fast your heart is beating. You can check your own pulse by counting the number of heartbeats from pulse points on your neck or your wrist in one minute. A newborn baby's heartbeat is pretty fast. It should beat more than 100 times in a minute. If it does, the baby receives a score of two. If it beats less than 100 beats in a minute, the baby receives a score of one. If the baby's heart is not beating at all, it receives a score of zero.

G stands for Grimace. This is a test of the baby's facial grimace and reflexes. To test a baby's reflexes the nurse will look at the way a baby responds to stimulation—a tickle or a stroke—of the bottom of its feet. If the baby coughs, sneezes, or pulls away, it is given a score of two. If it grimaces, or makes a face showing it does not like being bothered, it gets a score of one. If it does not respond to the touch at all, it gets a score of zero.

The second A stands for Activity. This is a test of the baby's muscle tone. Most babies move around, enjoying the freedom of being able to wave their arms and legs for the first time. If the baby is actively moving, it gets a score of two. If its arms and legs are flexed or sprawled out, it gets a score of one. If the baby is lying very still and not moving at all, it gets a score of zero.

R stands for Respiration. Respiration is another word for breathing. Right after a baby is born, its mouth and nose are suctioned to remove any fluid and mucus that is still there from before it was born. Most babies start to cry right away. After all, being born is quite a shock to their little bodies. To cry well, a baby must be able to take a deep breath. If the baby is breathing well

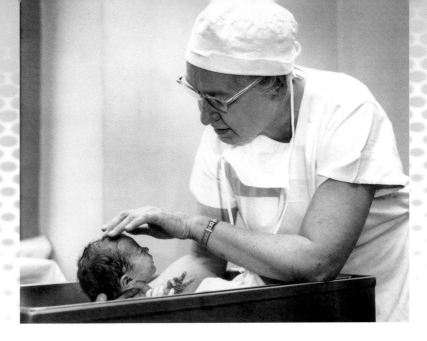

Virginia is pictured here checking one of her many infant patients for certain characteristics. It is important that newborns are breathing, moving, and responding properly to stimulation at birth.

and crying, it gets a score of two. If it is breathing slowly or seems to be having trouble breathing in a regular rhythm, it gets a score of one. If the baby is not breathing at all, it gets a score of zero.

It is easy to see that a baby who scores mostly twos is doing just fine. A baby who scores mostly ones might need to have some extra oxygen brought to its face. It might get a little

THE APGAR SCORE CHART

Below is a chart that is used to give each baby born in the United States an Apgar score.

	Sign	0 Points	1 Point	2 Points
A	Appearance (Skin Color)	Blue-gray, pale all over	Normal, except for extremities	Normal over entire body
P	Pulse	Absent	Below 100 beats per minute	Above 100 beats per minute
G	Grimace (Reflex Irritability)	No Response	Grimace	Sneeze, cough, pulls away
A	Activity (Muscle Tone)	Absent	Arms and legs flexed	Active movement
R	Respiration	Absent	Slow, irregular	Good, crying

tapping on its heels or a little rubbing to get it breathing better and moving more. A baby who scores mostly zeros is in big trouble. This baby needs emergency care. It may need a machine, called a ventilator, to help it breathe. It may need to have its heart started by the doctors. Most babies who have low or medium scores recover quickly with help. Others will have problems for the rest of their lives.

A LASTING IMPACT

The Apgar score is important because doctors and nurses have a standard way to evaluate babies' vital signs, and babies lives are saved. The Apgar score standardized the way all babies are checked out just after they are born. Originally, Virginia just meant for her score to check the babies at one minute after they were born to see whether they needed to be resuscitated. As the Apgar score became more widely used, however, doctors and nurses began to repeat the test at five minutes after birth. Then they could see whether a baby was getting better or worse. Eventually this led to the standard one- and five-minute Apgar score, which is still in use today all over the world.

The procedures that go on in the delivery room and immediately after birth are called neonatology. Modern neonatology owes a great deal to Virginia and her Apgar score. After she developed the Apgar score, Virginia moved on to do more research on things relating to newborn babies. She did important research about what bad things can happen if a baby does not get enough oxygen. She also did research to find out if anything bad happened to babies whose mothers had been given an anesthetic while the babies were being born.

5

Time for Hobbies

What Virginia loved most was practicing medicine and being a doctor. But there were plenty of other things that interested her as well. She had many hobbies that had absolutely nothing to do with her daily work as a doctor. Virginia was highly devoted to her work, but she never let her work drag her down. Nor was her work the only thing she did with her life. She had many other interests.

It's an interesting coincidence that one of Virginia's hobbies was stamp collecting. It would have made Virginia extremely happy to know that one day her own face would appear on a U.S. postage stamp.

Virginia took time out of her busy schedule to follow the Brooklyn Dodgers, shown here in 1952. Virginia was miraculously able to find time for her many hobbies even though her work as a doctor took up much of her time.

Virginia loved sports as well. In high school, Virginia had played basketball. In her adult years, Virginia preferred the quiet calm of playing a round of golf. She was also an avid baseball fan and rooted tirelessly for the Brooklyn Dodgers.

A LOVE OF LEARNING

Many people who knew Virginia Apgar have said one thing over and over about her: She was always learning. For Virginia, learning did not end when she graduated from school. For Virginia, the world was her classroom, and every day there was a new and exciting lesson to be learned. Even as an adult she was very curious. Dr. L. Stanley James, a professor emeritus of pediatrics and of obstetrics and gynecology, called Virginia "a student until the day she died." He said that, "Learning was the focal point of her life. Her curiosity was insatiable." This is a quality that people said helped Virginia stay young. Although she worked very hard all her life, she still made time for other things, too, such as her hobbies. She also made time to learn new things all the time.

Just a few years before Virginia died, she decided to try something very exciting. She had wanted to learn to fly an airplane, so she started taking flying lessons. She set a goal for herself, too. She wanted to fly under the George Washington Bridge in New York City someday.

TIME FOR FUN

Virginia was able to list lecturing as another of her many talents. She not only discussed her work but also told funny stories. Audiences loved to hear Virginia's lectures. In fact, she was so good at lecturing that she was asked to visit many different cities to give lectures on her work. It was a great way for Virginia to travel and see other parts of the world. She traveled a lot for work and she also found time to travel for fun. Because she traveled so often and to so many exciting places, Virginia had many chances to enjoy yet another one of her hobbies. Virginia loved angling. Angling is another word for fishing with a hook and a line. Virginia's extensive traveling fed her hobbies: Had she not traveled so much for work she might not have had so many chances to enjoy some of her hobbies. Virginia had the chance to enjoy angling in exotic places such as Australia's Great Barrier Reef and in the salmon rivers of Scotland. She loved deep-sea fishing as well.

Of all of Virginia's hobbies, however, her favorite had to be music. She grew up with music in her home and continued to find ways to express

Virginia valued her time off from work. She found time for her music, travel, and flying lessons. Here at the beach, Virginia shows off her relaxed side.

herself musically as she grew up. Even when Virginia was very busy working she thought it was important to make time for music. It is pretty amazing to think that, with all she had to do at work, she still had time to play her cello and viola in the Teaneck Symphony of New York, the Amateur Music Players, and the Catgut Acoustical Society. In fact, music was so important to Virginia that she almost always took either her cello or her viola or

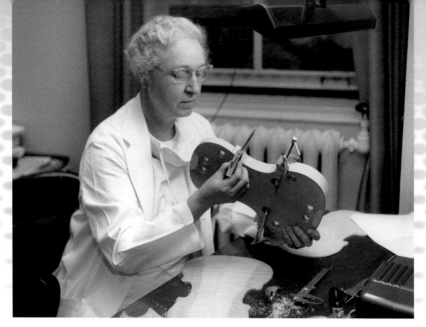

Virginia first got the idea to build her own instruments from Carleen Hutchins, a patient who brought one of her handmade instruments with her to the hospital before surgery. She and Virginia became friends, and Carleen shared her knowledge of instrument making with Virginia. Here, Virginia works on a violin.

both with her when she traveled. That way, she was able to practice her music when she had a bit of free time to relax during her busy schedule. She also had a chance to do something especially exciting with her music while she traveled. More than once she was invited to join different chamber music groups in the cities where she visited. Although she could not become a regular player with any of these orchestras, it was great fun for Virginia to visit and play music with them even if only for one night.

Virginia had played the violin since she was a little girl. As an adult she took her love of musical instruments even further. She was no longer content simply to play her own violin. Virginia was about to learn how to make stringed instruments herself. How this very busy woman found time for yet another hobby is a story of its own.

Making Instruments by Hand

In 1956, Virginia was visiting with one of her patients, a high school science teacher who was also a musician. The patient was a woman named Carleen Hutchins. Carleen was about to go to the operating room for surgery. Virginia was probably talking to Carleen about their shared hobby of music as a way to relax her before the operation. Carleen told her doctor all about her interest in how stringed instruments produced sound. She told her the story of how she studied stringed instruments in a laboratory in her own home. Based on what she had learned from studying other stringed instruments, Carleen had started to make her own stringed instruments.

Visiting Carleen before her surgery turned out to be a very significant moment for Virginia. Carleen had brought one of her handmade violins to the hosptial. She asked her doctor if she would like to try it out. There was Virginia, playing the violin right in her patient's hospital room! Virginia was impressed. She was very happy with the beautiful music she made with Carleen's violin. The sound was excellent. This sparked an idea in Virginia's mind.

Virginia decided that she could find time to design and make handcrafted stringed instruments herself. Carleen's operation went well, and soon she was able to return to normal life. Some time after Carleen left the hospital, she and Virginia began to study instrument making together, and Carleen taught Virginia what she already knew about making her own instruments. Virginia was very busy with work, so she had to sneak in time to work on her instruments. Her sleepy neighbors were not very happy with the time she chose. Virginia set aside time from midnight to 2 AM for making instruments in the bedroom of her apartment. Woodworking tools were everywhere and she even had a workbench. Her neighbors might have been impressed to know that, eventually, Virginia's late-night work resulted in a violin, a mezzo violin, a cello, and a viola.

THE GREAT "PHONE BOOTH CAPER"

Although Virginia took her work very seriously, she was known for her sense of humor and for knowing when it was time for fun and games. There is a funny story about Virginia and her instrument making. To those who knew Virginia, this story was known as the Phone Booth Caper.

Virginia always wanted to do things the best she possibly could. This included her hobbies. So when it came to instrument making, she wanted the wood she used to be the best, most beautiful wood she could find. In 1957, her friend Carleen found a beautiful piece of wood for Virginia to use. She thought Virginia would be so pleased. But there was a problem. Someone, or more accurately, some*thing* was already using the wood. The piece of wood was the shelf in a pay phone booth in the

Columbia Presbyterian Medical Center lobby. Of course, this maple shelf could not be removed. Or could it? Virginia and Mrs. Hutchins first tried to get the wood by asking for it. The hospital turned them down. So the two women had to try something more creative.

Virginia set to work making a new shelf to replace the one in the phone booth. She used cheaper wood and matched the color by staining it with wood stain. Virginia was actually successful in staining the new shelf to match the color of the old shelf exactly. She happened to talk to the owner of a hardware store near the hospital. He was able to give her the correct stain, which he had given to the hospital for the original shelf twenty-seven years earlier.

The women then smuggled their tools into the hospital in a suitcase. Late at night, with Virginia standing guard outside the phone booth, Carleen got to work inside the phone booth. If a night watchman happened to pass by, Virginia would tap on the phone booth door. Carleen was armed not only with her tools but with a supply of dimes so she could drop one into the phone and pretend to make a call whenever necessary.

Everything was going as planned until Carleen was ready to install the new shelf. Much to her surprise, the new shelf was too long. Although the new shelf was only a mere quarter of an inch too long, something had to be done, and fast, before it was discovered that the phone booth was without its shelf. Virginia continued to stand watch while Carleen dashed into the ladies' room. At one point a nurse passed by the bathroom. Imagine her confusion when she heard the sounds of Carleen sawing in the bathroom! A short time later, Carleen installed the new shelf, which now fit perfectly. The old shelf was put to use as the back piece of Virginia's viola. No one was the wiser. That is, no one knew until Virginia and Carleen's little secret was revealed . . . in the *New York Times!*

6

March of Dimes Birth Defect Foundation

Throughout her life, Virginia worked awfully hard. As do many people in jobs that cause high levels of stress, she needed a break. In 1959, she decided to take a sabbatical. For one whole year, Virginia would take a rest from her responsibilities as an obstetric anesthesiologist. Most people who take a sabbatical spend their time off traveling or writing, or just doing things that their normally busy schedules do not permit. But Virginia decided to go back to school. She signed up for classes at Johns Hopkins University in Baltimore, and within a year she had earned her master's degree in public health.

Virginia, here at her desk at the March of Dimes, dedicated much of her time to helping others. Her efforts at the March of Dimes helped the organization become much larger and able to help more people. She also helped raise awareness of different birth defects so that babies born with abnormalities could be cared for properly.

During her sabbatical and in the years afterward, she also continued to give lectures. Her main topic was birth defects. She gave lectures at Cornell University Medical College and Johns Hopkins School of Public Health.

When her year of sabbatical was over, Virginia decided not to go back to work as an obstetric anesthesiologist. She was ready to move on to something new. Her master's degree and her interest in helping newborn children, especially babies and children who were born with birth defects, helped her to make a decision about what to do next.

She went to work for the National Foundation for Infantile Paralysis. You may have heard of this organization by another name: the March of Dimes.

THE MARCH OF DIMES

The March of Dimes is an organization that helps babies and children. It is best known for its treatment and vaccines for a disease called polio. Founded on January 3, 1938, as the National Foundation for Infantile Paralysis, the March of Dimes (as it has been called since 1988) is now more than sixty years old.

The March of Dimes was set up because of a disease called poliomyelitis (more commonly known as polio and also once called infantile paralysis). Today there is a vaccine for polio and people no longer have to worry about getting it. But in 1938 there was no vaccine for polio. About 50,000 people per year were becoming paralyzed or dying because they were getting sick with polio. In 1938, President Franklin D. Roosevelt, who himself had been left partially paralyzed by polio years before, started the National Foundation for Infantile Paralysis. He wanted to take care of

Continued on page 72

President Franklin Roosevelt helped start the organization that later became the March of Dimes.

Continued from page 71

people who had been paralyzed by polio. Perhaps more important, he also wanted to help doctors find a vaccine for people so that no one else would have to suffer or die from polio. Thanks to President Roosevelt and the National Foundation for Infantile Paralysis, babies now receive a vaccine to keep them from getting polio, and polio has been wiped out.

After the National Foundation for Infantile Paralysis took care of the polio problem, rather than shut down they decided to tackle some of the other problems affecting babies. One of the big concerns at the time was simply that of babies' general health. Many babies were being born with birth defects and many of these babies died. The people at the National Foundation for Infantile Paralysis decided they would help pregnant mothers and parents of children with serious illnesses or birth defects. They would accomplish this by doing research on different birth defects, raising money to help babies and children born with birth defects, and providing education programs for parents and the general public.

ENTER VIRGINIA APGAR

Virginia joined the National Foundation for Infantile Paralysis in July 1959. But Virginia became more than just a member of this very important foundation. When she joined, she was made director of the Division of Congenital Malformations right away. Eight years later, she became director of Basic Research. One year after that, in 1968, she was made vice president of the March of Dimes. In 1973, she was promoted to the highest office of senior vice president for Medical Affairs. Virginia spent fifteen years as an executive of the National Foundation for Infantile Paralysis, whose name evolved over the years to the March of Dimes. During those years she did many important things. She worked very hard to raise money to support the work done by the March of Dimes. The March of Dimes board was impressed by her ability to get the money they needed for their programs. In fact, the March of Dimes grew from a small group to a nationwide organization because of the amount of money

Virginia was able to raise. She directed research programs that helped to discover the causes of many birth defects, the way to prevent certain birth defects, and the way to take care of babies born with birth defects. She also worked hard to get the public to support the March of Dimes. Another project she worked on helped to make the public aware of the different kinds of birth defects with which babies could be born. She became an educator of the public, helping parents to understand what they could do to prevent certain birth defects or how they could spot and treat different birth defects.

Before Virginia's time, babies born with birth defects were often hidden. This is a terrible thing to do to a baby. But at the time, people did not know very much about the causes of birth defects, and they did not know how to take care of babies and children who were born with serious problems. Today, most parents whose babies are born with physical disabilities work hard to bring them home and help them to live as normal a life as possible. Before public awareness, however, doctors usually told parents that they should take their babies to institutions and leave them there. Doctors would actually tell the parents to forget that they had ever had the baby. Things are very different today, in part because Virginia did a great deal to raise awareness of birth defects.

7

A Famous Woman

Nowadays it is not unusual for a woman to become a doctor. But in Virginia Apgar's day it was almost unheard of. Becoming a doctor made Virginia stand out among the women of her time. But she did so many more things in her life that made her a woman who stands out even today.

Virginia was a well-known doctor. She held important positions on the board of the March of Dimes, she liked to play music and build instruments, and she took flying lessons. She was awfully busy. It would seem as though she would not have time to do much else. But one year before she died, Virginia found time to show that she had yet another talent. That talent was book writing.

AN IMPORTANT BOOK: *IS MY BABY ALL RIGHT?*

In 1963, a paper Virginia had written was published. Ten years later, Virginia had written and published more than seventy papers about anesthesiology, resuscitation, and congenital abnormalities, which are abnormalities passed down from one or both parents or are developed before a baby is born. But she had not yet written a book. So, in the early 1970s, with the help of a woman named Joan Beck, who was an author and a columnist, Virginia wrote a very important book. The book was called *Is My Baby All Right?* This book soon became very popular with new parents and those about to have babies.

When Joan Beck's son and his friends were teenagers, they used to love preparing for Virginia to come over to the Beck home to visit or work

Virginia's job as an obstetric anesthesiologist helped ensure the safety and health of both mothers and their children. She continued helping people by writing books on important subjects, such as child rearing and birth defects. Her efforts touched many lives and her work continues to help people.

with Joan. Before Virginia would arrive, the boys would go to the library. There they would look up all sorts of interesting things. They hoped to find some bit of information or obscure fact that Virginia did not know. The boys would come back to the Beck house armed with their difficult questions. Each would take a turn at challenging Virginia, asking for the answers to their questions. Virginia got every one of the answers right. The boys simply could not stump Virginia Apgar.

Virginia is also credited with writing a book called *Down's Syndrome (Mongolism)*, although she did not exactly write this book. Virginia edited papers that had been presented at a conference about Down's syndrome (which, at that time, was still called mongolism) that was held from November 24 to 26, 1969. The New York Academy of Science published a book of these papers in 1970.

ACCOMPLISHMENTS AND AWARDS

Virginia's work had many important results. Babies who might have become sick or who might have been born with birth defects had a better chance at a healthy life thanks to Virginia's efforts. Many people and groups wished to honor Virginia for the hard work that she did on behalf of babies.

From 1941 to 1945, Virginia was elected to be the treasurer on the board of the American Society of Anesthesiologists (ASA). Serving on a board may not seem like such a big deal today. But in the 1940s it was a very big deal for Virginia for one simple reason: She was the very first female officer of the American Society of Anesthesiologists. She also received the ASA Distinguished Service Award in 1961.

An honorary degree is an academic degree that is given to a person who did not go to a specific university, but to whom the university wishes to give a degree because of his or her important work. Virginia Apgar was given five honorary degrees in her lifetime. The Women's College of Pennsylvania honored her with the degree of doctor of medical science in 1964 and Mount Holyoke College gave her a doctor of science degree in 1965. She was an honorary fellow of the American Medical Association and American College of Anesthesiology where, in 1951 and 1952, she served as chairperson of its board of governors.

Sometimes the honors Virginia was given were in the form of opportunities to do more important work by way of lecturing and teaching. In 1959, she was made lecturer in medicine at Johns Hopkins. That same year she also worked as a clinical professor of pediatrics at Cornell University in New York. She was also given the titles of honorary associate fellow of the American Academy of Pediatrics and associate fellow of the American College of Obstetricians and Gynecologists.

When an adult joins a group that is somehow related to his or her work, it is called a professional membership. Virginia had a professional membership in several professional groups: the American Association for the Advancement of Science, the American Society of Human Genetics, the Harvey Society, the Teratology Society, and the

Teratology is the study of birth defects. Virginia is well known for her work in this field. She raised awareness of birth defects and provided information about how to prevent them. In her lifetime, she became known around the world for her efforts to improve the lives of newborns, no matter whether they were healthy or ill.

Twenty-Five Year Club of Presbyterian Hospital of New York.

Virginia earned other great awards and honors during her lifetime. In 1960, she was awarded the Elizabeth Blackwell Citation for Distinguished Service to Medicine by a Woman from the New York Infirmary. From 1966 until 1971, she also served as an alumna trustee at Mount Holyoke College. This meant that Virginia was a member of the board that managed the affairs of the college. The *Ladies' Home Journal* honored Virginia as its Woman of the Year in 1973. A ceremony to present this honor to Virginia was televised for everyone in the United States to see. In 1973, while she was still holding the honor of Woman of the Year, Virginia was given the honor of being named lecturer in the Department of Genetics at the Johns Hopkins School of Public Health.

A LIFE OF FIRSTS

In addition to her famous Apgar score, one of the things that Virginia was so well known for was being the first woman to accomplish so much in the world

On January 31, 1960, Virginia (second from right) *was presented with the Elizabeth Blackwell Award. Elizabeth Blackwell herself is considered to be the first female physician in the United States. This award is presented to women who have performed outstanding service to humanity.*

In 1973, Virginia was presented with Columbia University's Gold Medal for Distinguished Achievement in Medicine from the College of Physicians and Surgeons. Here, she poses with Dr. Shih-hsun Ngai, Dr. Emanuel M. Papper, and Dr. Henrik Bendixen at the ceremony.

of medicine. When Virginia made the decision to become a doctor, the medical field was a field dominated by men. During Virginia's early years of work it still was. As the years went by, however, Virginia helped to change all that. She was the first woman to receive many honors, titles, and positions that in the past had always gone to men.

One example of this was when she received Columbia University's Gold Medal for

Distinguished Achievement in Medicine from the College of Physicians and Surgeons in 1973. She was the first woman to win this award. In 1994, the American Academy of Pediatrics honored Virginia's memory by starting an award in her name. It is called the Virginia Apgar Award in Perinatal Pediatrics.

Of course, Virginia's most impressive honor (aside from the U.S. postage stamp and her induction into the Women's Hall of Fame, which both happened after she died) is one that has no official title. It was one she earned simply by doing her work and being very dedicated to that work and to the patients for whom she cared. Virginia changed the way the medical world evaluated newborns. By doing so, she paved the way to better health for babies and children, giving them the best chance for the best start they could hope for. Virginia's most important role, the way she is most often remembered, was as a leader in the prevention of birth defects. She was thought of this way not just in the United States, but internationally as well.

8

The End . . . and After

Late in her life, Virginia had another special patient to care for. Virginia took care of her mother, who lived in the same apartment building Virginia lived in, until March 16, 1969. That day, when Virginia was sixty years old, her mother died and Virginia lost her most special patient.

Just five years later things took another bad turn. Summer was drawing to a close. Virginia was living in Tenafly, New Jersey. Although she was still very active and extremely busy, Virginia's body would not keep up and she fell ill. She was admitted to Columbia Presbyterian Medical Center in New York. She lay in a bed that was probably once occupied by patients of her own. This time Virginia was the patient, and her doctors were unable to make her well again.

AN UNTIMELY END

On August 7, 1974, Virginia Apgar died of progressive cirrhosis of the liver, from which she had been suffering for a few years. She was only sixty-five years old. It is hard to imagine that such a vital, young-at-heart, energetic woman died at such a relatively young age. A few years before she died, Virginia had stomach surgery, most likely due to the cirrhosis. But whether this operation had anything to do with her death is not known. What is known is that when Virginia died, the world lost a truly amazing woman, and the world of medicine lost a trailblazing pioneer. But Virginia would not soon be forgotten.

Virginia was buried beside her parents in the Fairview Cemetery in Westfield, New Jersey. Also nearby is a gravestone showing the dates of a sadly short life: September 3, 1900, to April 22, 1904. This is where Virginia's brother, Charles

After her death, Virgina was remembered as an important force in the field of medicine. Here, she and Dr. Bongiovanni examine a newborn infant. The advent of the Apgar score will forever tie Virginia to the well-being of newborn babies.

Emory Apgar Jr., who died so many years before, is buried. Virginia's gravestone is marked with the words "Creator of the Apgar Score."

Of Virginia's immediate family, only her brother Lawrence—who retired from a long musical career first as a professor of music at Western College for Women in Oxford, Ohio, and then as a professor of musicology at Earlham College in Indiana—was still alive. Lawrence was retired and living in Pocono Lakes, Pennsylvania, when his famous sister died. Lawrence died in 1988. It is Lawrence's grandson, Eric Apgar, who spoke on behalf of the Apgar Family at the Women's Hall of Fame induction.

A POSTAGE STAMP

Unfortunately, Virginia Apgar did not live to see her face on a postage stamp. In 1994, twenty years after she died, her portrait was pictured on a twenty-cent stamp, the stamps that were used to mail postcards. Certainly Virginia would have been excited to see her image on a postage stamp. Although she was not alive to experience this great honor, she might have been especially happy about it because she had enjoyed stamp collecting since she was a young girl!

It is quite an achievement to have your image featured on a postage stamp. So whose idea was it to put Virginia's face on a stamp? A pediatrician in Colorado named Dr. L. Joseph Butterfield (the same doctor who came up with the acronym APGAR) thought Virginia's lifetime achievements had earned her great honor. The University of Colorado professor of pediatrics became chairman of the committee that led a campaign to have a U.S. postage stamp created with Virginia's face on it. Beginning in 1980, Dr. Butterfield started a campaign to get Virginia honored on a postage stamp. Many newspaper and magazine articles were written about Dr. Butterfield's campaign. People who did not know about Virginia and her Apgar score before knew about it then. People all across the country were reading about her life and the wonderful things she had done to help prevent birth defects in babies.

VIRGINIA APGAR

It took ten years of hard campaigning, but at last Dr. Butterfield and his committee's efforts paid off. Finally, the idea to honor Virginia with a postage stamp was approved. The date was set. At the annual meeting of the American Academy of Pediatrics in Dallas, Texas, on October 24, 1994, Virginia Apgar's very own postage stamp was unveiled. Virginia was one of only two anesthesiologists to get their face on a U.S. postage stamp. (The other anesthesiologist was a doctor named Crawford Long.) People who attended this special unveiling at the American Academy of Pediatrics meeting were treated to a bit of entertainment. A string quartet of musicians played music. This was no ordinary string quartet, though. They played some of Virginia's favorite music. Even more special, though, were the instruments they played. One of the musicians played a cello that Virginia had made. Two of the musicians played violins she had helped to make. And the fourth musician in the quartet played a viola she had helped to make. The quartet had a fitting name, too: They called themselves the Apgar Quartet.

HALL OF FAME

Virginia Apgar's great-nephew Eric was there when Virginia was inducted into the National Women's Hall of Fame in Seneca Falls, New York. Twenty-one years had passed since Eric's great-aunt had died. But on Saturday, October 14, 1995, Virginia Apgar was one of eighteen important women to be inducted into the National Women's Hall of Fame. With Virginia's induction, the number of women in the National Women's Hall of Fame reached 125. Virginia was certainly in good company. Some of the other women in the Hall of Fame are Susan B. Anthony, Rosa Parks, Senior Congresswoman Patricia Schroeder from Colorado, the famous jazz singer Ella Fitzgerald, and U.S. Supreme Court Justice Sandra Day O'Connor, to name just a few.

Although Eric was only ten years old when her great-aunt Virginia died, as a grown man he still remembers her and is proud of her many accomplishments. Eric was honored to represent his family and give a speech about Virginia at the ceremony that day.

This medal would have been presented to Virginia, had she been alive at the time of her induction into the National Women's Hall of Fame. Over twenty years after her death, Virginia's hard work was still affecting people.

Virginia Apgar was an amazing woman. In just sixty-five years she became a well-respected doctor, a musician, a musical instrument maker, a world-renowned lecturer, and the creator of a world-famous test to help babies. She won many awards and honors. She was well liked by friends and well respected by colleagues. She was admired for her great contributions not only to science but to society as well. She lived a happy life of working hard, yet always made time for things that interested her.

Her work was groundbreaking and paved the way for women in a world that had been dominated by men. Virginia Apgar's achievements and success set a standard for the things that any woman can do if she really puts her mind to it. Virginia Apgar's success and achievements set a standard for women all over the world.

TIMELINE

1909 On June 7, Virginia Apgar is born to Helen Clarke Apgar and Charles Emory Apgar in Westfield, New Jersey.

1925 Virginia enters Mount Holyoke College, majoring in zoology.

1936 The nurse anesthetists at Columbia Presbyterian Hospital begin teaching Virginia the basics of anesthesiology at a time when there were no physician anesthesiologists at the hospital.

1939 Virginia receives her board certification from the American Society of Anesthesiologists. She is the second woman to get this diploma.

1949 Virginia becomes the first woman with a professorship in anesthesiology at the College of Physicians and Surgeons at Columbia University.

1953 Virginia's Newborn Scoring System is first published.

1959 Virginia joins the National Foundation for Infantile Paralysis (now known as the March of Dimes) as director for the Division of Congenital Malformations.

1959	The American Society of Anesthesiologists presents Virginia with their Distinguished Service Award.
1962	Two pediatricians from the University of Colorado Medical Center come up with the term "Apgar score" as the new name for Virginia's Newborn Scoring System.
1973	Virginia is named Woman of the Year by *Ladies' Home Journal* magazine. She is featured on national television for this honor.
1973	Virginia receives the Gold Medal for Distinguished Achievement in Medicine from the College of Physicians and Surgeons, Columbia University. She is the first woman to win this award.
1974	On August 7, Virginia Apgar dies in New York City at the age of sixty-five.

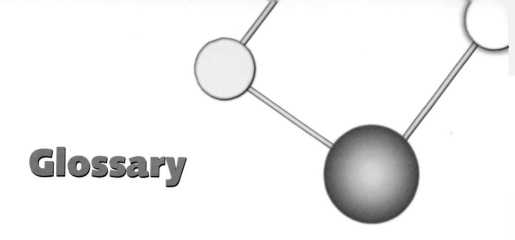

Glossary

acronym A word formed by using the first letters of a group of words.

anesthesia A loss of feeling with or without a loss of consciousness.

anesthesiologist A doctor responsible for giving anesthetic to patients.

anesthetic Medicine that causes a loss of feeling or consciousness.

angling Recreational fishing with a hook and a line.

chronic Continuing for a long time or returning often.

congenital Resulting from heredity or prenatal development.

eczema A disease that causes the skin to be red, itchy, and covered in scaly or crusted spots.

Glossary

fellowship A sum of money paid from an endowment to support a graduate student.

genetic Passed down from one or both parents.

honorary degree A degree that is given to a person who did not go to a specific university, but to whom a university wishes to give a degree because of his or her important work.

internship A time when graduates of medical school get practical experience in a hospital.

neonatology A branch of medicine that deals with the period of time just after a baby is born.

obstetrics A branch of medicine that deals with the care of women while they are pregnant, during the delivery, and afterward.

perinatal The period of time just before and just after a baby is born.

residency Serving a full-time position at a hospital.

resuscitation To bring back to life by performing emergency medical procedures.

sabbatical A period of time spent away from one's job.

VIRGINIA APGAR

treasurer The person responsible for handling the money and finances of a group or an organization.

trustee A person who has been given legal responsibility for someone else's property.

zoology The branch of biology that deals with animals and animal life.

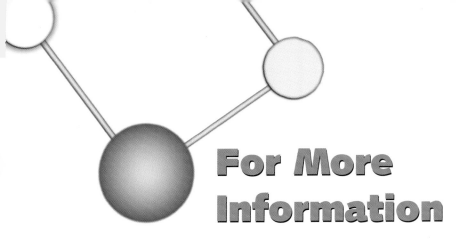

For More Information

American Society of Anesthesiologists
520 N. Northwest Highway
Park Ridge, IL 60068-2573
(847) 825-5586
Web site: http://www.asahq.org

**Columbia University College of Physicians
and Surgeons**
630 West 168th Street
New York, NY 10032
Web site: http://cpmcnet.columbia.edu/dept/ps

March of Dimes Birth Defects Foundation
1275 Mamaroneck Avenue
White Plains, NY 10605
(888) MODIMES (663-4637)
Web site: http://www.marchofdimes.com

VIRGINIA APGAR

National Women's Hall of Fame
76 Fall Street
P.O. Box 335
Seneca Falls, NY 13148
(315) 568-8060
Web site: http://www.greatwomen.org

WEB SITES

Due to the changing nature of Internet links, the Rosen Publishing Group, Inc., has developed an online list of Web sites related to the subject of this book. This site is updated regularly. Please use this link to access the list:

http://www.rosenlinks.com/whfms/vapa

For Further Reading

Apgar, Virginia, and Joan Beck. *Is My Baby All Right?* New York: Simon & Schuster, 1972.

Hacker, Carlotta. *Nobel Prize Winners*. New York: Crabtree Publishing, 1998.

Keenan, Sheila. *Scholastic Encyclopedia of Women in the Unites States*. New York: Scholastic, Inc., 2002.

McClure, Judy. *Healers and Researchers: Physicians, Biologists, Social Scientists*. New York: Raintree Steck-Vaughn, 2000.

Stille, Darlene R. *Extraordinary Women Scientists*. Chicago: Children's Press, 1995.

Wyatt, Valerie. *The Science Book for Girls and Other Intelligent Beings*.Toronto: Kids Can Press, Limited, 1993.

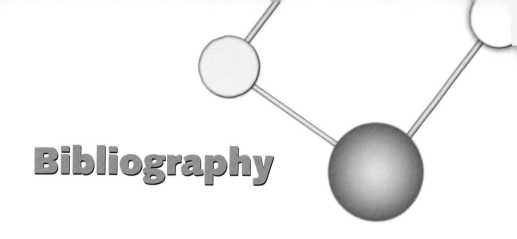

Bibliography

Apgar Family Association, Inc. Retrieved February 2002 (http://www.apgarfamily.com).

Calmes, Selma Harrison, M.D. "Virginia Apgar: A Woman Physician's Career Is a Developing Specialty." *Journal of the American Medical Women's Association,* Vol. 39, 1984, pp. 184–188.

Calmes, Selma Harrison, M.D. "Virginia Apgar, M.D.: At the Forefront of Obstetric Anesthesia." *ASA Newsletter*, October 1992, pp. 9–12.

Enocha, Bonita Eaton. "Virginia Apgar: A Legend Becomes a Postage Stamp." *P&S Journal*, Vol. 14, No. 3, Fall 1994.

Eric Apgar's Family Web Site. Retrieved February 2002 (http://apgar.net/virginia).

Rose, David W. March of Dimes Resource Center. "March of Dimes Biographical Note: Virginia Apgar Papers, 1921–1994 finding guide." 1994.

Rupreht, Joseph, M. J. Van Lieburg, W. Erdmann, J. A. Lee, eds. *Anaesthesia—Essays on Its History*. Berlin: Springer-Verlag, 1985.

"Virginia Apgar." Who Named It? Retrieved February 2002 (http://www.whonamedit.com/doctor.cfm/204.html).

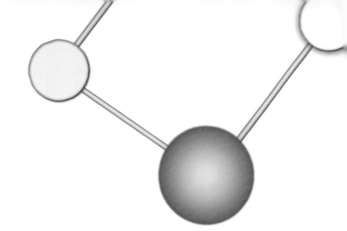

Index

ACKNOWLEDGEMENTS
With much gratitude and thanks, the author gratefully acknowledges the assistance of Eric Apgar, Judy Hankinson of the Apgar Family Association, Inc., and Dr. Selma Calmes, without whom this book would not be the tribute that it is.

ABOUT THE AUTHOR
Melanie Ann Apel has written more than thirty books for the Rosen Publishing Group. This is her first biography. Melanie has a degree in theatre arts from Bradley University and a degree in respiratory care from National-Louis University. Melanie lives in Chicago with her husband Michael Bonnell and their perfect baby boy (Apgar scores of 9 and 8!).

DESIGN AND LAYOUT
Evelyn Horovicz

SERIES EDITOR
Eliza Berkowitz